101 BEST OPENING LINES

101 BEST OPENING LINES
(MEETING PEOPLE)

ERIC WEBER

Harmony Books/New York

Published by Harmony Books, a division of Crown Publishers, Inc., One Park Avenue, New York, New York 10016 and simultaneously in Canada by General Publishing Company Limited

HARMONY and colophon are trademarks of Crown Publishers, Inc.

Portions of this book have been previously published in slightly different form in *100 BEST OPENING LINES.*

Manufactured in the United States of America

Library of Congress Cataloging in Publication Data

Weber, Eric, 1942–
101 Best Opening Lines

1. Dating (Social customs) 2. Interpersonal communication. I. Title.
HQ801.W59 1983 646.7'7 82-21223
ISBN 0–517–54954–9

10 9 8 7 6 5 4 3 2 1

First Edition

INTRODUCTION

THINK ABOUT IT. You probably have a chance to meet hundreds of new people every day. But most of us are shy, afraid to approach someone we don't know and start a conversation. Nobody likes to be rejected, and this fear stops us from putting ourselves in a vulnerable situation. And so, we never take the chance. There are two reasons why you shouldn't let your fears keep you from trying to meet people.

First, if you try to start a friendly, non-threatening conversation with someone, the possibility that you will be rejected is very slim. Remember that most people are just like you—they want to make fun, interesting, new friends. They are not sitting there alone at a party (or in a bar or a club) waiting to reject everyone who comes along. The average person loves to talk and will love to talk to you, *if given a chance.* Look at it this way:

You have your good points and your bad points, like everyone else. (You know all the "bad" things about yourself and often assume that others will, too.) You are scared because of your insecurities. But studies have shown that, during first meetings, people tend to stress your *good* qualities rather than your so-called "bad" ones. (You probably find yourself doing the same thing with others.)

Second, *rejection is not that bad.* Imagine that you see someone sitting alone on a couch at a party. You sit down, open with a brilliant conversation starter, and the object of your desire looks at you and says, "Get lost." There, that's it. Your worst fears have come true. *So what?* It's not your fault. That person may not want to respond to you for any number of reasons unrelated to you. But it's OK. The chemistry might not be right, but that doesn't make you any less of a person. It's their problem and their loss. They missed a chance to know you, and you are probably one of the most interesting people you know. There are plenty of other people to meet—just try again.

Why do we want to meet new people, especially of the opposite sex? To start relationships. Although not every conversation will become a relationship, every relationship starts with a conversation. The search for companionship is the reason for most of the socializing that goes on all over the world. An important point: Don't think that meeting someone new and having a good conversation always has to lead to a "one-night stand." This attitude will cripple your chances. People will pick up on it, and this will turn most of them off immediately. Concentrate on meeting someone new and unique and maybe even seeing that person again.

That is where this book comes in. You are at a club, and you see someone across the room you would like to meet. The first thing to do is make eye contact. If the attraction is there, eye contact will be held a fraction of a second longer than if it is just an inadvertent glance in your direction. It will be barely perceptible, but you will feel it. If you fail to make eye contact the first time, try again. If you fail repeatedly, the other person is either too shy to meet your gaze or just does not want to meet you. Phew! You've spared yourself a rejection already. Try someone else.

Once you have made successful eye contact, smile slightly. The other person will almost always smile back. Now is the time to act. You must make your way over to them and say something. You will be prepared.

Use one of the simple and witty lines in *101 Best Opening Lines.* How about this one? "I'm writing a book on opening lines. What would work with you?" (Line 59). Or "Why don't you let me buy you a double? By the time you finish it you'll really think I'm witty" (Line 28). Or even "Those jeans look better on you than they do in the ads" (Line 43). You have 98 more conversation starters that cover almost any situation. These lines are suggestions that you can use verbatim, or as starting points, or as ideas for other conversation starters. Once you've started talking, the other person will make things a lot easier by continuing the conversation and giving you more things to say. And there you are.

Which brings us to an important element in meeting people: Self-confidence. Most of us don't have as much of it as we'd like. But that's OK. *101 Best Opening Lines* will boost your self-confidence by giving you charming conversation starters to get you over the toughest part of meeting someone—the opening line.

Remember: These lines are nonthreatening. The person you are meeting has probably had it up to here with come-on lines. You are trying to give something of yourself, not get something.

So good luck, and keep in mind, you have to say *something* to get started. The rest of this book is conversation starters, some general, most built around common situations. And they work—you just have to go out there, be confident, don't worry about rejection, and you'll be fine.

Editor's note: Most of the lines in this book will work equally well for males or females and are labeled (M/F). Some of the lines are specifically targeted for one sex and are labeled (M) for male only and (F) for female only.

THE LINES

1.

A LIFESAVER

In a snowstorm (M/F)

“On a day like this, we need a Saint Bernard to come along with some brandy.”

Natural events like snowstorms seem to bring people closer together—people battling the elements appreciate companionship. And since a dog is not likely to come along, how about the nearest bar?

2.

GOING MY WAY?

On an elevator (M/F)

“If I'd known we were going to take this long, I would've brought my pajamas.”

Everyone hates slow elevator rides, and misery loves company. Also, you have a captive audience.

3.

SCHOOL DAZE

In class (M/F)

“You seem to take really good notes. Could I compare them with mine?”

Or say you missed a recent lecture. This request is very difficult to refuse and, of course, you have the class to talk about already.

4.

LOVE THY NEIGHBOR

At the incinerator (M/F)

“I see we have the same taste in trash.”

This line can be very witty when you are both throwing your garbage down the chute. It also works at some gallery openings.

5.

THE GO-AHEAD

On the street (M/F)

"I could never get over my Boy Scout/ Girl Scout training. May I help you across the street?"

Use this line next time you're waiting for a light at a busy intersection.

6.

WHO WANTS TODAY'S PAPER?

Anywhere (M/F)

"Would you like a section of my newspaper?"

Here's a line that can be used on subways, buses, park benches, in hotel restaurants and lobbies, in waiting rooms, and at airports and train stations—in short, anywhere people read newspapers.

7.

SUBWAY SWITCH

On a bus or subway (F)

"You look like you've had a tough day; why don't you take my seat?"

A good turnaround of a traditional situation and an impossible request to refuse.

8.

TAKING CARE OF BUSINESS

At a business convention or seminar (M/F)

"Hello. I'm Joe/Sue Smythe of General Grain."

Nonthreatening and acceptable behavior. Everyone really goes to conventions to meet people anyway.

9.

LADY LUCK

Buying a lottery ticket (M/F)

"Would you buy a lottery ticket for me? You have that lucky look about you."

Complimentary, nonthreatening, and the thrill of gambling is romantic.

10.

A BETTER VIEW

In a high-rise apartment building (M/F)

"Do you face the mountains or the city (the river or the park)?"

Good elevator conversation for meeting all those neighbors you see constantly walking in and out but have never talked to.

11.

SAME TIME, NEXT DAY

At lunch, outdoors (M/F)

"Well, I really enjoyed talking to you. Shall we do it again tomorrow, say around twelve-thirty?"

This line is for those times when you eat your lunch on the steps of the library (or in the park) next to someone you've been aware of all through lunch but haven't said anything to. Cute and charming.

12.

GOOD NEWS TRAVELS FAST

At the newsstand (M/F)

"You're the best news I've seen all day."

Given the headlines of the times, this may not always be that extraordinary a compliment. But delivered with conviction, it should certainly be enough to flag someone's attention.

13.

SINGIN' IN THE RAIN

In a rainstorm (M/F)

"Would you like to share my umbrella?"

A classic. Who could refuse? And you have a good opportunity to make nonthreatening physical contact—there's rarely enough room for two under an umbrella. Variation: "Why don't you come in out of the rain?"

14.

SHINING NIGHT

On the street at night (M)

"You shouldn't be walking here alone at night. It's dangerous. May I escort you home?"

This line works best for men. Be very friendly and careful in your approach as the woman may think you are one of the neighborhood dangers you are warning her against. Don't try it in New York City. But it's very gallant.

15.

WINDOW-SHOPPING

Outside a department store (M/F)

“I bet you’d look sensational in that.”

That’s probably what someone looking at clothes in a store window is wondering about, so you’ve answered a mental question and given a compliment at the same time.

16.

DOG DAYS

On the street (M/F)

“Excuse me, could I see that newspaper after you’re done with it?”

Say this line to someone cleaning up after their dog with a newspaper. Borderline-sick, but it will probably get a laugh from most people (if only from embarrassment). Try to follow up quickly with further witticisms.

17.

HEAVYWEIGHT

On the street (M/F)

“Here, let me help you carry those things.”

Everyone appreciates a sincere offer of help. And you wind up together at the front door.

18.

IT’S ACADEMIC

In a bookstore (F)

“My, a gentleman and a scholar.”

Use this line when you see a man leafing through an interesting book. Complimentary, charming, and erudite.

19.

COPYCAT

At the Xerox copier (M/F)

“I'd like to make a copy of your face to take home with me.”

The Xerox copier has replaced the water cooler as the best meeting place in the office. This comment is so bizarre the recipient probably won't be able to keep from laughing. Next you can talk about how much you both hate Xeroxing.

20.

A FLASK OF BRILLIANCE

On a ski slope (M/F)

“How about a little brandy to warm you up?”

Carry a flask with you while skiing and offer it to someone while both of you are shivering and waiting for the lift. Variation on the classic, “May I buy you a drink?” (see line 78), with the added warmth of brandy in the cold.

21.

A RUNNING RELATIONSHIP

At the track (M/F)

“Would you mind timing me for a quarter-mile?”

A good line if you are a fast quarter-miler (can be embarrassing otherwise). Afterward you can discuss running shoes, foot problems, shin splints, and all those other riveting subjects that crop up when runners shoot the bull.

22.

ALL WET

On the beach (M/F)

“Come on in. I’ll be your buddy.”

Buddy is a double entendre playing on the “buddy system” in swimming, with the second meaning in this case signifying friend. That’s an awfully nice offer to make to someone who’s probably had it up to here with sleazy, salacious remarks.

23.

ASK FOR HIS HAND

Anywhere (F)

“Could you give me a hand with this please?”

When you are carrying something heavy. Traditional, but difficult to refuse. See line 17 for reverse situation.

24.

TENNIS ANYONE?

At the tennis court (M/F)

“You must be the pro here.”

A great compliment, even if not true. You can follow up with: “I’d like to play with you, but I’d probably end up with love.”

25.

BABY, HOLD ONTO ME

In a health club (M/F)

“Would you hold my legs down while I do my sit-ups?”

Establishes physical contact, but nonthreatening at the same time.

26.

AN HOUR LATER, YOU WANT MORE

At a Chinese restaurant (M/F)

“That's just what I wanted to get. How about me ordering some sizzling shrimp and then we can share?”

No one likes to eat alone (see lines 27, 31), and Chinese food is a natural for sharing. It's also more fun when you take out.

27.

A LURING LUNCH . . .

In a restaurant (M/F)

“Why don’t you sit here? I hate to eat alone.”

When the restaurant is full and you have an empty seat at your table.

28.

DOUBLE VISION

In a bar (M/F)

“Why don’t you let me buy you a double? By the time you finish it, you’ll really think I’m witty.”

A witty variation on “May I buy you a drink?” (see line 78). Good irony about yourself and a traditional situation (and probably true).

29.

HAPPY HOUR

In a bar (M/F)

“Look! You made my ice cubes melt.”

Probably anyone you say this line to is going to be a little confused as to how. Explain that just sitting close by has caused your temperature to rise so that the ice in your drink melted. Say it all with a big smile. A great way to break the ice.

30.

BETWEEN BITES

At a luncheonette (M/F)

“If this place had a liquor license, it would have been a champagne cocktail.”

Use this line after sending the waitress over to the person you want to meet with a Coke, Tab, Perrier, etc. Sending someone a drink is a very classy way to meet.

31.

BENEATH THE ARCHES

In MacDonald's (M/F)

"Haven't we McMet before?"

Unless this person has wandered into MacDonald's from Jupiter, this line will seem at least mildly amusing, in which case you can ask if you may share the table. Later, say that next time you have lunch together, you'd like to go someplace really special—like Burger King.

32.

IT'S A BARGAIN

At the flea market (M/F)

"You look like an expert. Is this stuff really worth fifty dollars?"

Flattering, and you can continue to browse together.

33.

HIGHBROW TALK

In the campus library (M/F)

“I’m writing a paper on the methodology of initiating interpersonal communication. Let’s talk.”

Let’s face it, hardly anybody goes to the library to study. Pseudo-intellectualism is always good for a laugh.

34.

ART LOVER

In a museum (M/F)

“You look like a French Impressionist painting.”

Try to read a little about Impressionism before using this line. Museums are prime places for meeting people, Impressionism is a very popular period, and you have hours of ready-made conversation ahead of you.

35.

AT SOMEONE ELSE'S EXPENSE

On an elevator

"See what happens when you eat too much?"

An enormously obese person steps off the elevator. After the doors close, you turn to the person you want to meet and point out the perils of overeating. A bit cruel, perhaps, but can be funny if delivered correctly.

36.

A CUTTING LINE

At the hairstylist (M/F)

"I hope you gave your hairdresser a big tip. You look terrific!"

That's what anyone who's just had a haircut wants to hear—and *you* said it.

37.

BANK ON IT

On line in the bank (M/F)

“At this rate I'll bet they're printing the money in the back room.”

Not only are you both stuck on line, but you are about to get money (great to have on dates). This line is especially effective on payday, when everyone hates the bank even more for only having two tellers working.

38.

THE INTERIOR DECORATOR

At the paint store (M)

“How do you think these colors would look in my living room?”

Use this line while holding up samples of green and orange. No one will think they match. Ask for help choosing a better combination. Vulnerability is cute.

39.

A LITTLE BIT COUNTRY

Anywhere (M)

“You look like a country girl.”

An unusual, nonthreatening compliment. Follow up with remarks about “peaches-and-cream complexion.” Substituting “boy” doesn’t quite work, so this one is for men only.

40.

A TASTY TREAT

In the bakery (M)

“How does a pastry lover like you stay so thin?”

Almost all women want to be thin (see lines 75, 82 for variations). Also plays on their guilt at being in a bakery.

41.

LITERARY LINE

In a bookstore (M/F)

“Do you know anything about this book?”

Meat-and-potatoes line. Nothing fancy, just a good solid opening. And you've established that you *read books.* You're already a prime catch.

42.

DRESSED TO KILL

In a department store (M/F)

“You look about his/her size. Would you help me choose one of these?”

A classic. You're buying that shirt/dress for your brother/sister. If you're adventurous, buy the item for your model if you hit it off.

43.

OOH, LA LA . . .

In a department store (M/F)

"Those jeans look better on you than they do in the ads."

We can't all be Brooke or the Sergio man, but who doesn't want to?

44.

PETTING

In a pet store (M/F)

"See the puppy with the circle around his eye? He likes you."

This one is as cute as they come. Be ready to buy the dog if called upon.

45.

COOKIN'

At the butcher shop (M/F)

"I'm tired of cooking these the same old way. Do you have a new recipe I could try?"

Everyone has a favorite recipe. Variation: "If I buy these, will you cook them for me?"

46.

MEAT COUNTER

At the butcher (M)

"Excuse me, but how long do you fry a roast beef?"

You don't fry a roast beef, you roast it. Frying will ruin it. Once again, cute vulnerability—maybe she will offer to cook it for you (see line 45 for variation). Follow up with: "Do you live around here?" Most people do live near their supermarkets.

47.

IN VINO VERITAS

In a liquor store (M/F)

“If you’re looking for a good Bordeaux, this one tastes very much like a ’64 Chateau Margaux at about one-third the price.”

Finding the right wine can be a problem; help is sure to be appreciated. Study up on your wines before trying this one.

48.

MIXED DRINKS

At the supermarket (M/F)

“Did you ever mix these two together? It’s fantastic!”

Use this line while pointing to bottles of orange juice and Listermint or Diet Pepsi and Wesson Oil. The Steve Martin effect.

49.

SHOPPING AROUND

At the supermarket (M/F)

"By the time we get to the register, the prices will probably go up again!"

Everyone likes to complain about prices, and this line should be timely for quite a few years.

50.

WASH LINE

In the Laundromat (M/F)

"Is a cup of this stuff enough?"

Use this line as you are about to pour a cup of silver polish or Mop & Glo into your wash. Anyone with even the most rudimentary knowledge of washing will realize that you are about to make a grave error and want to help. You can explain that you thought "cleaners were cleaners" and worked on just about anything.

51.

GEARING UP

On a bike (M/F)

“Wanna race?”

When you pass someone you want to meet while you are riding your bike. Simple.

52.

PLANE TALK

On an airplane (M/F)

“I can’t wait until this plane lands in Rio.”

Use this line on any domestic flight. The correct response is “But this plane is only going to Chicago.” You can then reply, “But from there we can catch a connecting flight to Brazil.” Extremely romantic.

53.

FRIENDLY SKIES

At the airport (M/F)

“My man is waiting. Can I give you a hand?”

After you give your bags to a redcap and tell him to wait, use this line on someone with a ton of luggage. Lots of snob appeal here.

54.

A BUS LINE

On a bus (M/F)

“You know, I’ve been riding this bus to work for two months now, and this is the first time there’s been someone interesting to sit next to.”

Buses are so boring. Also works on subways, airplanes, trains, etc.

55.

SEAT WITH A VIEW

On a commuter train (M/F)

“If you sit with me, I’ll let you have the window seat.”

Works well with people you see every day but haven’t talked to.

56.

NO TYLENOL, PLEASE

Anywhere (M/F)

“You wouldn’t happen to have an aspirin with you by any chance?”

An all-time classic. Evokes sympathy and makes you seem totally nonthreatening. Follow up with an explanation—a hangover, up all night working on your novel, tension over meeting a new client—all give you a chance to say something good about yourself.

57.

A LINE FOR THE WORLD

Anywhere (M/F)

“Hi. You look nice. My name is Joe/ Sue.”

Right to the point.

58.

DANCING THE NIGHT AWAY

Anywhere (M/F)

“Excuse me. Are you a dancer?”

Flattering—and an invitation to go dancing is a natural follow-up.

59.

PULITZER PRIZE–WINNING LINE

Anywhere (M/F)

“I’m writing a book on opening lines. What would work with you?”

Witty and original.

60.

A NOVEL IDEA

Anywhere (M/F)

“I’d like to model my novel’s heroine/ hero after you. Would you tell me your life story?”

This line is terrific for several reasons. It’s clever and a compliment at the same time. Also gives you both plenty to talk about—your writing and their life.

61.

A PERFECT MATCH

Anywhere (M/F)

"A match? How about you and me?"

Try this line when somebody asks you for a match. Corny enough to get a laugh. Note: Keep your Bic ready in your pocket and practice a smooth delivery—very impressive.

62.

PARTY POSSIBILITIES

At a party (M/F)

"I just want you to know that I've been here for fifteen minutes, studying everybody in the place. (Pause for a moment.) **No one even comes close to you."**

Takes nerve, but this line is to the point and if the person addressed is interested, it will start things off right.

63.

WHAT A RACKET!

Anywhere (M/F)

“You know, I can tell from just looking at you that you must be a terrific tennis player.”

Try this line on someone carrying a tennis racket. If you are right they will be impressed by your sports acumen. If not, they will be flattered. Follow up with a suggestion that you play sometime. (Works best if you do play tennis.)

64.

STOP! IN THE NAME OF LOVE

On the street (M/F)

“Stop! Wait right here until I can think of something to say.”

Establish eye contact first, as stopping people on the street can be risky. Good for those just-not-to-be-missed people you see on the street. Try to have a good follow-up ready.

65.

SPRINGTIME

In the park (M/F)

"On such a beautiful day, I feel I just have to make new friends."

Simple and true.

66.

HELP FROM ABOVE

Anywhere (M/F)

"I wish we were going to Paris together in that plane."

Use this line when you see a plane overhead and someone you'd like to meet down below. Paris is the most romantic city in the world. Keep a small bag packed, just in case.

67.

THE CALL OF THE WILD

At the zoo (M/F)

“I don’t usually talk to strangers, but this place brings out the animal in me.”

Also works well in crowded subways.

68.

COMPATIBILITY TEST

At the coat check (M/F)

“Our coats have just spent two hours together. Why don’t we have a brandy and see if we’re just as compatible?”

Also works at the dry cleaners.

69.

STAR QUALITY

In a restaurant (M/F)

“You’re an actor/actress, aren’t you?”

Here’s a line that might not work all that well in Hurdsfield, North Dakota, but in a large city it can work very well in those trendy, artsy restaurants where all the waiters and waitresses are actually aspiring thespians.

70.

PAINLESS DENTIST

At the dentist’s office (M/F)

“With a smile like yours, he should use you in his ads.”

A trip to the dentist is often anxiety-filled, and a great compliment like this one is a sure-fire conversation starter.

71.

SPACE WARRIORS

At the video arcade (M/F)

"I couldn't have done it without you for good luck."

Try this line after a particularly stunning display of skill. Maybe you can invade Mars together with your next quarter.

72.

SPECIAL DELIVERY

In the post office (M/F)

"At the speed the mail is delivered, I feel I should be wishing this letter 'Bon Voyage.'"

Then you can discuss the horrors of the U.S. mails (good for hours of conversation).

73.

A MATTER OF LIFE OR BREATH

Anywhere (M/F)

"I know that if we tried together, we could both give up smoking."

Best if both you and the person you want to meet are smoking.

74.

JUICY FRUIT

In the supermarket (M)

"You look like you know about these. Can you tell me if this is ripe?"

Say this line while holding up cantaloupes (oranges, etc.). Try it on women wearing halter tops. Be prepared for a slap.

75.

LOVE IS A MANY-FLAVORED THING

In an ice-cream store (M/F)

“I wish I could get away with two scoops.”

Complimentary, and everyone is calorie-conscious in an ice-cream parlor.

76.

TOAST OF THE TOWN

In a bar/restaurant (M/F) Nonverbal

Catch the eye of someone you want to meet, and raise your glass in a toast.

Follow up by sending a drink over. Very sophisticated.

77.

IRISH EYES ARE SMILING

Anywhere (M/F)

"You must be Irish (Italian, French, etc.)."

Works both ways—even if you are wrong, explain why you thought so, in most complimentary terms.

78.

MAY I? . . .

In a bar (M/F)

"May I buy you a drink?"

The all-time classic. You are offering something in exchange for the privilege of meeting the person (see lines 20, 28, 30 for variations).

79.

BRIEF ENCOUNTER

Anywhere (F)

“Nice suit (nice tie, etc.).”

Complimentary and opens the door for further discussion.

80.

LET'S SPLIT

At a bus stop (M/F)

“Would you like to split a cab?”

Great during those endless waits for a bus. You're already going in the same direction, and it probably won't cost much more. Also works if you've both reached a cab at the same time.

81.

CHAMPAGNE KICKS

In a bar (M/F)

“I’ll bet you a glass of champagne I can guess your name.”

You guess wrong, and you’ve bought a drink.

82.

. . . AND ONLY ONE CALORIE

In a supermarket (M)

“Oh c’mon, you don’t need that.”

Try this one on a woman buying a Tab or a Weight Watcher’s dinner. Implication: You don’t need diet food (see lines 35, 40, 75 for variations).

83.

ELEVATED INTRODUCTION

On an elevator (F)

“Excuse me, your pocket flap’s getting wrinkled.”

Or, “you have a thread hanging, a button open,” etc. Your helpfulness will be much appreciated.

84.

SONY, NO BALONEY

Anywhere (M/F) Nonverbal

Mouth the words “Hello beautiful/Hello handsome” to somebody wearing a Walkman.

How to start a conversation with someone wearing a Walkman. The problem of the eighties.

85.

ON THE SCENT

Anywhere (M/F)

“What is that perfume/cologne you’re wearing?”

It’s wonderful! Where did you get it? . . . and so on.

86.

AFTERNOON DELIGHT

At the office (M/F)

“Let’s have lunch.”

Lunch dates are the least threatening and least committal of all dates. A good way to meet new people at work.

87.

WHERE AM I?

On the street (M/F)

"Can you please direct me to the Algonquin?"

Even if you know where it is. Try to ask someone walking in the same general direction, and then walk with them. Choose any classy place, and see if they will join you for a drink.

88.

FORTY WINKS

On a train (M/F)

"Could you please wake me up at my stop?"

Sit down next to someone you want to meet, say this line, and doze (or appear to) for a few minutes. Then wake up, yawn, and begin talking.

89.

FRIEND OF A FRIEND

At a party (M/F)

“Who do you know here?”

Many people at parties don’t know anyone there. If they don’t, you can follow up with “Let’s leave then.” If they do know someone, you have something in common to talk about.

90.

YOU REMIND ME OF . . .

Anywhere (M/F)

“I’m sure you hear this all the time, but you look amazingly like John Irving/ Jane Curtin.”

Try to choose a celebrity with at least some resemblance and be subtle; stay away from Robert Redford or Raquel Welch comparisons.

91.

ROLE REVERSAL

Anywhere (F)

“What’s a nice man like you doing in a place like this?”

Cute turnaround of *the* clichéd opening line. There are numerous variations on this theme.

92.

TIE-ING ONE ON

In a store (F)

“Did you get that tie here?”

It’s really attractive, etc. Shows you have the same taste in ties and stores.

93.

BREAKING THE ICE

At a skating rink (M/F)

"Can you teach me how to skate backward?"

Or, if you already know how, offer to teach someone. Fun and establishes easy physical contact.

94.

GENERAL HOSPITAL LINE

In a hospital cafeteria (M/F)

"After looking at my pot roast, I've decided I'd better sit close to someone who knows the Heimlich maneuver."

Someone like a doctor or a nurse.

95.

MATA HARI TIME

On the street (F)

“Can you walk with me? I think I'm being followed.”

Intriguing and exciting. Try to be obviously tongue-in-cheek so you don't come off as a paranoid.

96.

NUMBER ONE

In a record store (M/F)

“Wouldn't it be great if they had a dance floor here?”

When a “hot” song comes on while you are looking through the racks next to someone you'd like to meet.

97.

SAY CHEESE

Anywhere touristy (M/F)

"I'm not camera shy."

When you see someone who is obviously a tourist. Offer to take their picture in front of something memorable. If there is more than one person, offer to pose with the one you want to meet.

98.

MIRROR, MIRROR

In a store (M/F)

"That really looks great on you."

Whenever you see someone trying on something. Your helpful opinion should be much appreciated.

99.

HOW'S YOUR LOVE LIFE?

Anywhere (M/F)

"You really love life, don't you?"

Whenever you see someone doing something with obvious gusto.

100.

POPPING THE QUESTION

At the movies (M/F)

"Would you like to share my popcorn?"

A much more fun way to watch a movie. Remember the scene in *Diner?*

101.

HERE'S LOOKING AT YOU, KID

Anywhere (M/F)

"We'll always have Paris."

The most romantic line ever, from the most romantic movie ever. Best if delivered in an unusual situation.

About the Author

ERIC WEBER, the world's foremost authority on meeting people, is the author of the best-selling *How to Pick Up Girls, How to Win Back the One You Love, The Shy Person's Guide to a Happier Love Life,* and *Separate Vacations,* a novel.